P9-EJJ-338

EXPLORING THE WORLD OF

Seals and Walruses

Tracy C. Read

FIREFLY BOOKS

A FIREFLY BOOK

Published by Firefly Books Ltd. 2011

First Printing

Publisher Cataloging-in-Publication Data
(U.S.)
Read, Tracy C.
    Exploring the world of seals and
    walruses / Tracy C. Read.
[   ] p. : photos. ;   cm.
Includes index.
ISBN-13: 978-1-55407-784-7 (bound)
ISBN-10: 1-55407-784-2 (bound)
ISBN-13: 978-1-55407-797-7 (pbk.)
ISBN-10: 1-55407-797-4 (pbk.)
1. Seals (Animals) -- Juvenile literature.
2. Walrus -- Juvenile literature. I. Title.
599.74/5 dc22   QL737.P64R433   2011

Library and Archives Canada
    Cataloguing in Publication
Read, Tracy C.
  Exploring the world of seals and walruses /
Tracy C. Read.
Includes index.
ISBN-13: 978-1-55407-784-7 (bound)
ISBN-10: 1-55407-784-2 (bound)
ISBN-13: 978-1-55407-797-7 (pbk.)
ISBN-10: 1-55407-797-4 (pbk.)
  1. Seals (Animals)--Juvenile literature.
  2. Walruses--Juvenile literature. I. Title.
QL737.P6R42 2011   j599.79
C2010-907684-2

Published in the United States by
Firefly Books (U.S.) Inc.
P.O. Box 1338, Ellicott Station
Buffalo, New York 14205

Published in Canada by
Firefly Books Ltd.
66 Leek Crescent
Richmond Hill, Ontario L4B 1H1

The publisher gratefully acknowledges the financial support for our publishing program by the Government of Canada through the Canada Book Fund as administered by the Department of Canadian Heritage.

Cover and interior design by
Janice McLean, Bookmakers Press Inc.

Manufactured by Printplus Limited in Shen Zhen, Guang Dong, P.R.China in January, 2011, Job #S101200439.

Front cover: © Wayne Lynch
Back cover: © Andrea Leone/Shutterstock
Back cover, inset, left: © Wayne Lynch
Back cover, inset, right top:
   © Jeff Grabert/Shutterstock
Back cover, inset, right bottom:
   © Witold Kaszkin/Shutterstock

CONTENTS

BETWEEN MEALS

A California sea lion basks in the warm sun before heading out on its next fishing trip.

MEET THE PINNIPEDS

Humans are designed for life on land, and those of us who can swim know how it feels to spend hours in a pool or lake. No matter how sunny the day or how warm the water, we eventually get chilly and uncomfortable. Imagine, then, what it would be like to spend weeks at a time in the frigid sea, constantly searching for food and watching for fierce predators like sharks and whales.

Seals, sea lions and walruses — all known as pinnipeds because they have fins, or flippers, instead of feet — are able to do just that. Over millions of years, they have evolved physically to meet the harsh demands of life in the water. Yet most of these marine mammals leave the water to mate and give birth, so they must be equipped to survive on land or ice as well.

There are 33 species of seals worldwide, and nearly a dozen of them make their home in the coastal waters of North America. These seals come in a wide range of sizes and colors and exhibit a variety of different behaviors, though they are all carnivores, which means their primary food is meat. The pinnipeds are divided into three subgroups: the eared, or otariid, seals, which include the sea lions and fur seals; the earless, or phocid, seals; and the walrus, the only surviving member of its family, Odobenidae.

Let's find out how these pinnipeds meet the challenges of life in the sea and on land.

4

FORM & FUNCTION
Like this very round harbor seal, all seals are basically torpedo-shaped. It's the most effective form for moving through the water at a steady pace.

ANATOMY LESSON

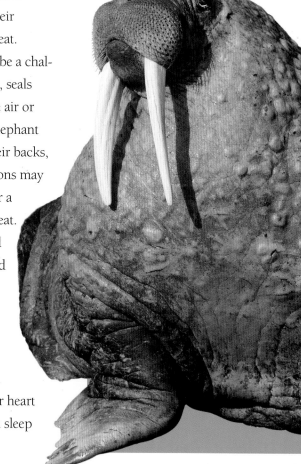

Powerful flippers, a torpedo-shaped body, a long flexible neck and spine and reduced or nonexistent external organs allow the streamlined seals, sea lions and walrus to navigate their aquatic world.

But seals often have to adjust to extreme temperatures, both in and out of the water. The earless seals and walrus have a thick layer of blubber to keep them warm in icy polar waters, while eared seals rely on an insulating fur coat. Seal flippers act as a heat exchanger, shunting warm or cold blood to other parts of the body, and seals resting in the cold water may hold their hind- and foreflippers above the water to conserve heat. On-shore, sea lions, elephant seals and walruses find warmth in numbers, huddling in their colonies to share body heat.

Staying cool can also be a challenge. On a sunny beach, seals wave their flippers in the air or dip them in the water. Elephant seals flip wet sand on their backs, while fur seals and sea lions may slip off to a shady cave or a tide pool to escape the heat.

With more blood and more oxygen-carrying red blood cells than most land mammals, seals are adapted for long, deep dives. They can reduce their heart rate while still supplying oxygen to their heart and brain. Seals can even sleep underwater.

THE NAKED AND THE FURRED
A thick, knobbly hide over a layer of blubber protects the walrus (facing page) from the icy waters. With a profile described as "squashed in," the northern fur seal stays warm with an outer coat of guard hairs over a dense, waterproof underfur.

PINNIPED PROFILES
The California sea lion pup (right), an eared seal, has tiny external ear flaps; the harbor seal (center) is an earless seal, with a small ear hole on each side of its head. The one-of-a-kind walrus (far right) lacks external ears but has major-league teeth, or tusks.

Weighing up to 2,000 pounds (907 kg), the male Steller sea lion is the largest of the eared seals; the female weighs half that. Its whiskers are 20 inches (51 cm) long.

Teeth
Cone-shaped pointed teeth enable the seal to grip slimy, squirming prey.

Whiskers
A seal's sensitive whiskers pick up vibrations from passing fish.

The stretch factor
By rotating its front flippers and stretching, a seal can scratch an itch almost anywhere on its body.

Eyes
With modified eyelids and no eyelashes, the seal's eyes produce gobs of protective mucus. A membrane acts like a windshield wiper to clear sand and salt from its eyes.

Relaxed approach
Having no collarbone allows the seal to be more flexible both in the water and on land.

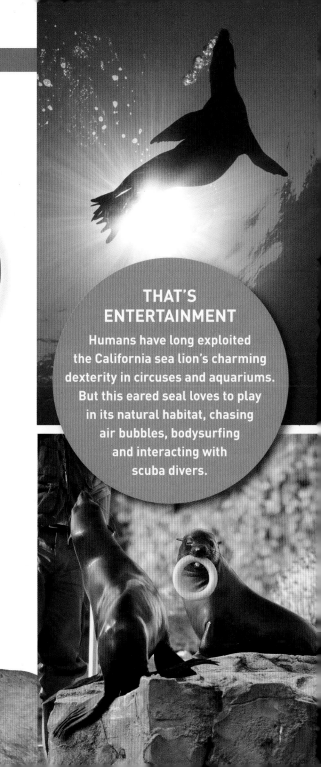

Born to swim

The earless seal counts on its fan-shaped rear flippers to propel it in the water, using its front flippers for steering. Adapted for life in the water, most earless seals are awkward on land.

Special features

Relative to its body length, the seal has the longest intestine in the world. One Steller sea lion's intestine measured 264 feet (80 m).

Flipper power

Paddle-shaped front flippers power the eared seal through water, while its rear flippers help it walk and run on land.

THAT'S ENTERTAINMENT

Humans have long exploited the California sea lion's charming dexterity in circuses and aquariums. But this eared seal loves to play in its natural habitat, chasing air bubbles, bodysurfing and interacting with scuba divers.

NATURAL TALENTS

The evolution of the seal to a life lived almost entirely in the water has required trade-offs — its ease and comfort on land, for one. But this marine mammal displays some remarkable natural talents in both habitats.

When underwater, for instance, a specially constructed inner ear allows the seal to receive and filter sound from all directions. Its highly sensitive hearing helps it pinpoint the location of prey, predators and other seals.

While the seal's underwater hearing is exceptional, it doesn't hear as well on land as do other land carnivores. Still, it can distinguish sound and the direction from which it is coming, which gives it an advantage when searching for its family members or detecting threats.

With its big round eyes, a seal can see well both in the water and on land. (The walrus, with its relatively tiny eyes, relies instead on its long whiskers to forage in the dim light on the ocean floor.) In murky underwater light, well-developed muscles allow the pupils of the seal's eyes to enlarge and, therefore, gather more light. In the bright, burning sunlight reflected from snow and ice, its pupils contract to vertical slits to keep harmful light out.

A protein membrane of keratin (the same material from which our fingernails and hair are made) protects the seal's eyes both in the water and out, while

EYES PEELED

A walrus (facing page top) takes a break from combing the ocean floor for food, while a ringed seal (facing page bottom) and a California sea lion (above) show off their big light-gathering eyes.

another layer of tissue guards against the water pressure the seal is exposed to during deep dives. Finally, extremely active tear ducts keep the eyes well lubricated, and inner eyelids wipe away salt and sand.

Well-developed hearing and vision may offset the seal's poor sense of smell underwater, where it closes its nostrils. On land, however, it's a different story. Researchers report that a seal can detect a human hundreds of feet away, and a mother seal carefully nuzzles her pup to identify and imprint its unique smell.

It is believed that seals do not enjoy an elaborate sense of taste.

The seal's world is one filled with touch, and whiskers are an important part of that. Of varying lengths and characteristics, whiskers are a vital tool for all pinnipeds, for both foraging and navigation. And anybody who has seen a colony of sea lions, walruses or elephant seals piled on top of one another knows that these pinnipeds love to press the flesh.

SEA HUNT
When the weather is harsh at the surface, the harbor seal spends most of its time underwater, ever alert for a fish dinner.

SMELL
A seal has a keen sense of smell on land, but it closes its nostrils underwater.

SIGHT
A seal's large round eyes are adapted for both low light levels underwater and bright sun.

HEARING
While excellent underwater, a seal's hearing is slightly less so on land.

TASTE
It all tastes like fish to the seals.

TOUCH
Its whiskers gather information, and many seal species seem to enjoy snuggling with family and friends.

GONE FISHING

Worldwide, pinnipeds live in a range of aquatic habitats, from polar ice caps and the equatorial Galapágos Islands to freshwater lakes, temperate coastal areas and open ocean.

The eared seals (Otariidae family) that make their homes along the western coast of North America include the northern fur seal (which spends most of the year in the open waters of the North Pacific) and the Steller sea lion and California sea lion, both of which tend to stick close to the coastline. These seals do not occupy the frozen waters of the Arctic.

Some of the northern earless seals (Phocidae family) that inhabit the harsh Arctic environ-ment include the ringed seal, the harp seal, the bearded seal and the hooded seal. The harbor seal is likewise found in the High Arctic but roams as far south as southern California and along the east coast, while the gray seal is limited to the rocky coasts and cliffs south of the Arctic and north of Cape Cod. The northern elephant seal, also earless, prefers warm temperate waters and ranges along the western coast of North America.

The walrus lives on both sides of the continent, in the Arctic waters of the northern Pacific and Atlantic oceans.

No matter where they are found, however, the pinnipeds share a common taste for food

ICE MACHINES

The earless seals that live in the frozen Far North, such as the harp seal (facing page bottom), have larger claws than the eared seals living in ice-free zones — the better to chop breathing holes in the ice. The bearded seal (below and facing page top) uses its head to bash holes in the ice.

items. Fish of all kinds, including salmon, trout, herring, sardines, flounder, smelt and cod, mollusks, such as squid, octopus and clams, and a shrimplike crustacean called krill are all on the hit list.

Still, it's not always fish for dinner. Some northern seals occasionally feed on other seals. Male Steller sea lions have been observed preying on northern fur seals, harbor seals and ringed seals, often pups or juveniles, while male walruses sometimes dine on young bearded seals and ringed seals. Seals may even snatch up the odd seabird for a quick meal.

Since so many of the pinnipeds forage out at sea — and down deep in the sea — there is a lot we don't know about their feeding habits, which can also vary depending on the season and the seal's gender and age.

We do know that seals adapt to their circumstances — working solo, with partners or in small groups or gathering in a large herd to hone in on a huge school of fish. Steller sea lions in Alaska have been seen leaving the shore in the daylight to fish in a massive group numbering in the thousands. Yet they also hunt singly at night.

Solitary fishermen, like northern fur seals, migrate where their dinner takes them, spending many months at sea and feeding on squid and fish such as herring, salmon and rockfish.

The most unique foraging style belongs to the walrus. It uses the more than 600 whiskers on its upper lip like fingers, feeling its way over the ocean floor and rooting around like a pig in the mud for clams and crabs and other bottom-dwelling creatures.

Seals have also earned a reputation as fish thieves. Grabbing up trout at the mouth of freshwater streams or breaking into fishing nets to snack on trapped fish has not endeared them over the years to the commercial fishing industry.

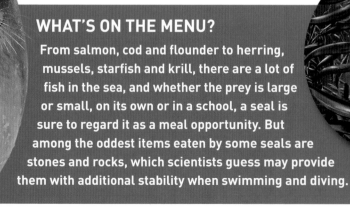

WHAT'S ON THE MENU?

From salmon, cod and flounder to herring, mussels, starfish and krill, there are a lot of fish in the sea, and whether the prey is large or small, on its own or in a school, a seal is sure to regard it as a meal opportunity. But among the oddest items eaten by some seals are stones and rocks, which scientists guess may provide them with additional stability when swimming and diving.

CALIFORNIA DREAMIN'

Hauling out to laze in the sun, these California sea lions may also do a little dockside fishing.

'HAREM SCAREM'

Seals don't have a single — or simple — approach to mating. Researchers believe that much depends on where seals start their families. Some species breed on land, some on ice that is attached to land and others on free-floating ice in the Arctic.

Land-breeding seals (including the northern elephant seal, the northern fur seal, the gray seal and the California and Steller sea lions) haul out in large numbers on islands or remote beaches, where they can best avoid land predators. With secure real estate hard to find, the females, or cows, are forced to gather together in colonies, creating an opportunity for one male to defend and breed with a number of them. This sys-tem is called polygyny, and the females are known as a harem. The male, or bull, is considerably larger than the females, some-times comically so.

Each year, the males return to the same breeding site. Some set up territories before the females arrive, while others establish their power over competing males through ferocious displays of strength and size. The elephant seal bull, for instance, starts the season bulked up with blubber and ready to fast for two to three months while he guards his territory and breeds with as many females as he can.

Ice-breeding seals tend to have just one mate per year, a system called serial monogamy. The

FREE LOVE

For many male seals, more is better when it comes to breeding partners. They bully and bash their way to the top of the colony using size and strength and enjoy the benefit of offspring without the hassle of child care.

REACH FOR THE TOP

Among the gray seals (facing page top), northern elephant seals (facing page center), walruses (facing page bottom) and Steller sea lions, shown sunning themselves on a rocky outcrop (above), the males are always significantly larger than the members of their harems.

TOUGH LOVE
After 10 to 12 days, the mother harp seal abandons her pup (left). It must live off its new blubber until it exchanges its white coat for a gray coat (right) and learns to swim and feed itself.

females can spread out near a breathing hole (and food source) in the ice and are not dependent on a male for protection. Generally speaking, these males and females are about the same size.

Once again, the walrus is the exception. Gathering in huge herds on the Arctic ice, the strongest walrus bulls compete for the attention of the females with courtship displays of vocalization and tusk size.

Whatever the breeding system, however, there is one consistent detail in every seal's family life: Once the mating season is over, the male's job is done.

Typically, the female seal gives birth to one offspring roughly a year after breeding, usually in early spring, when food sources for the mother are more plentiful.

The kind of care a pup receives depends on where it is born. Land-born pups are nursed on nutritious milk from their mothers over several months, gradually growing until they are able to find food for themselves. A mother and pup identify each other through scent, and the mother protects her pup from the many dangers of a crowded colony, including being crushed. During this period, the mother goes off on occasional foraging trips.

Pup seals born on ice, on the other hand, have a short, intense childhood. These pups enter a cold, dangerous world. Their mothers may try to give birth in a sheltered spot or on fragile ice avoided by predators like the polar bear and arctic fox. Still, the clock is ticking. The mothers do not feed as they nurse their young with rich, fat-filled milk for periods that range from a few days to several weeks. The award for shortest childhood goes to the hooded seal. In three to five days, this pup doubles its birth weight of 48 pounds (22 kg) and is then deserted by its mother.

On land or ice, though, a pup's first year is filled with risk.

LAND & ICE

The land-born northern fur seal pup, above, is nursed by its mother for four months, the harbor seal pup (below left) for around a month. The mother of the Arctic-born hooded seal pup (below right) says good-bye after only a few days.

HABITAT HAZARDS

Seals pay another price for a double life spent on land and in the sea: They are vulnerable to predators and other perils in both settings.

In the Far North, seals are a prized menu item for the polar bear, which has devised strategies for dining on several species. A powerful swimmer built to spend long hours in freezing water, the polar bear can hunt its prey in the sea and on the icy land. It may quietly approach a seal stretched out in the sun or wait beside a hole in the ice for one to come up to breathe. (An old Inuit myth claims that the polar bear has been seen throwing chunks of ice at walruses to injure or kill them.)

A range of northern carnivores, including coyotes, wolves and arctic and red foxes, also stalk seals — especially pups and juveniles — on land and ice. Even aggressive ravens have been known to attack a seal pup.

In the water itself, sharks and killer whales pose a particular hazard. Looming up from the inky depths of the ocean, a great white shark can seize a young seal in its mighty jaws. A single whale may rush into shallow water to nab a pup, while organized pods of whales present an even bigger threat.

Humans, predictably, deliver the greatest harm. We kill seals for their meat and fur, even as we poison and destroy their habitats.

OCEAN SOS

Humans continue to work overtime to damage the planet's oceans. Sewage, toxic waste, garbage, oil spills and global warming combine to threaten the habitat and health of all marine animals, including pinnipeds.

PHOTOS © SHUTTERSTOCK
p. 3 Colette3
p. 7 top: VasikO
p. 7 bottom center: Bruce Raynor
p. 8 naturediver
p. 9 top: Natalie Jean
p. 9 bottom: Jo Chambers
p. 12 Andrea Leone
p. 13 Jeff Grabert
p. 14 bottom: Vladimir Melnik
p. 16 right top: Joe Belanger
p. 16 right bottom: Joy M. Prescott
p. 17 slowfish
p. 19 Linda Hughes
p. 20 right: AleksandrN
p. 21 bottom left: Anyka
p. 21 bottom right: Gentoo Multimedia Ltd.

PHOTOS © ISTOCKPHOTO
p. 16 right middle: Nikontiger
p. 18 top: micmayhew
p. 22 top: Petek Arici
p. 22 bottom: Brasil2
p. 23 top: Tom Barrat
p. 23 bottom: Håkan Karlsson

PHOTOS © WAYNE LYNCH
p. 5
p. 6
p. 7 bottom left
p. 7 bottom right
p. 10-11 all
p. 14 top
p. 15
p. 16 left
p. 18 middle
p. 18 bottom
p. 20 left
p. 21 top